Titles in the Amazing Working Dogs with American Humane Series

FIRE DOG HEROES
ISBN-13: 978-0-7660-3202-6

GUIDE DOG HEROES
ISBN-13: 978-0-7660-3198-2

POLICE DOG HEROES
ISBN-13: 978-0-7660-3197-5

SEARCH AND RESCUE DOG HEROES
ISBN-13: 978-0-7660-3201-9

SERVICE DOG HEROES
ISBN-13: 978-0-7660-3199-9

THERAPY DOG HEROES
ISBN-13: 978-0-7660-3200-2

AMAZING WORKING DOGS with

AMERICAN HUMANE
Protecting Children & Animals Since 1877

POLICE DOG HEROES

Linda Bozzo

Bailey Books
an imprint of
Enslow Publishers, Inc.
40 Industrial Road
Box 398
Berkeley Heights, NJ 07922
USA
http://www.enslow.com

This book is dedicated to Officer Shawn Meade and his brave K-9 partner, Lucky who are both assets to the community in which they work.

Founded in 1877, the American Humane Association is the only national organization dedicated to protecting both children and animals. Through a network of child and animal protection agencies and individuals, American Humane develops policies, legislation, curricula, and training programs—and takes action—to protect children and animals from abuse, neglect, and exploitation. To learn how you can support American Humane's vision of a nation where no child or animal will ever be a victim of abuse or neglect, visit www.americanhumane.org, phone (303) 792-9900, or write to the American Humane Association at 63 Inverness Drive East, Englewood, Colorado, 80112-5117.

AMERICAN HUMANE

Protecting Children & Animals Since 1877

Bailey Books, an imprint of Enslow Publishers, Inc.

Copyright © 2011 by Enslow Publishers, Inc.

Library of Congress Cataloging-in-Publication Data

Bozzo, Linda.
    Police dog heroes / Linda Bozzo.
       p. cm. — (Amazing working dogs with American Humane)
    Includes bibliographical references and index.
    Summary: "The text opens with a true story of a police dog, and then it explains the history of the K-9 unit and the training methods used to transform an ordinary dog into a canine hero"—Provided by publisher.
    ISBN-13: 978-0-7660-3197-5
    ISBN-10: 0-7660-3197-7
    1. Police dogs—Juvenile literature. I. Title.
    HV8025.B64 2010
    363.2'32—dc22
                                      2008048017

Printed in China

052010 Leo Paper Group, Heshan City, Guangdong, China.

10 9 8 7 6 5 4 3 2 1

To Our Readers: We have done our best to make sure all Internet Addresses in this book were active and appropriate when we went to press. However, the author and the publisher have no control over and assume no liability for the material available on those Internet sites or on other Web sites they may link to. Any comments or suggestions can be sent by e-mail to comments@enslow.com or to the address on the back cover.

Every effort has been made to locate all copyright holders of material used in this book. If any errors or omissions have occurred, corrections will be made in future editions of this book.

Illustration Credits: Associated Press, pp. 28, 38, 40, 44; Shaun Best/Reuters/Landov, pp. 1, 3, 34; Nicole diMella/Enslow Publishers, Inc., pp. 6, 8, 10-11; © Cheryl Ertelt/Visuals Unlimited, pp. 20, 22; © Seth Gottfried, p. 39; Library of Congress, p. 16; © Military Stock Photography, p. 36; www.photos.com, p. 14; David L. Ryan/Boston Globe/Landov, p. 31; Shutterstock, pp. 15; James R. Tourtellotte/MAI/Landov, p. 24; Jeanne White/Photo Researchers, Inc., p. 26.

Cover Illustration: Shaun Best/Reuters/Landov.

Contents

Thank You

Enslow Publishers, Inc. wishes to thank Edgar R. "Eddie" Brannon Jr. of the American Working Dog Association for reviewing this book.

The author would like to thank Officer Shawn Meade and the Edison Township (N.J.) Police Department for all of their cooperation.

K-9 Lucky
A True Story

It is a cool autumn evening. Leaves are just beginning to fall in Edison, New Jersey. Officer Shawn Meade, with K-9 Lucky in the backseat, is patrolling the streets of this usually quiet town. Then they receive a call.

A woman was robbed at a nearby train station. The robber has fled the scene. Lucky must help find him.

The night is quiet when they arrive where the

robber was last seen. Officer Meade straps on Lucky's harness and leash. "Do you want to go to work?" he asks the dog. "Do you want to catch the bad guy?"

Lucky replies with a bark. Wasting no time, Lucky puts his nose to the ground. He begins sniffing for a human scent. Suddenly, a noise comes from the yard of a nearby house. Walking toward the noise, Lucky barks again. They are surprised to see a man crawling out from under a porch. Officer Meade orders, "Lie down on the ground!" But the man stands up. He walks toward them. Lucky barks even louder. Officer Meade tries again. "If you don't get down I will let my dog go!" The man still refuses.

Feeling threatened, Officer Meade releases Lucky from his leash. He gives the command, "Go get him!" Before Lucky reaches him, the man does a smart thing. He is terrified of what Lucky might do

Officer Shawn Meade stands with K-9 Lucky.

to him. He raises his hands in the air. "I give up." In a loud voice, Officer Meade orders, "No! Lucky come! Come, come, come!" Lucky obeys. Instead of attacking the man, the dog returns to his partner's side. "Good boy," Officer Meade praises Lucky.

Officer Meade hooks Lucky back on his leash. This time the man follows the officer's orders. He lies down on the ground. "Watch him," Officer Meade tells Lucky while he searches the man for weapons. Lucky barks at the man to let him know he is watching him. Officer Meade radios for help from other officers.

When the other officers arrive, the man is handcuffed. Officer Meade praises Lucky for doing a good job. He repeats, "Good boy. Good boy." He pats Lucky on the head.

K-9 Lucky is a hero!

But Lucky's job is not done. Officer Meade and Lucky return to the scene of the crime. They need to find the victim's purse. This is called an article search. "Seek, fetch!" Officer Meade commands. Lucky uses his keen sense of smell to search for a fresh human scent. He covers the area using a zigzag pattern while sniffing the ground. Not only does Lucky find the victim's purse, he is able to find her cell phone and wallet on the nearby train tracks. Lucky is rewarded at the end of his search with his favorite chew toy for a job well done. K-9 Lucky is a true canine hero.

Chapter 1

The History of Police Dogs

umans and dogs have worked together for thousands of years. This relationship was first limited to herding cattle and sheep and guarding property. Later, dogs were used on patrol for protection.

In Saint Malo, France, dogs were used on patrol as early as the 1300s. These protected the townspeople. This practice continued until the late 1700s.

France organized its police dog program as

early as 1770. Belgium and Germany followed with their police dog programs. In 1897, German policemen often worked alone. This was especially dangerous when they were on night patrol. Unfortunately, there was no money to hire additional officers. Something needed to be done. Police inspector Franz Laufer thought the answer might be dogs. In October 1901, the inspector put his first police dog on patrol. The dog was a Great Dane named Caesar. The work of these first police dogs was to protect officers on patrol. Later, they were trained to perform other tasks, such as tracking.

Ghent, Belgium, was the

The first school for police dogs was in Ghent, Belgium. Police officers trained different types of dogs.

first city to start a school for police dogs. The Ghent dog program started in early 1899 with three Belgian sheepdogs. Seven more were added soon after. These first dogs were trained for police work. Before the end of the year, thirty-seven dogs assisted ten members of the city's police force.

Great Danes were one of the first police dogs!

Soon, the use of police dogs spread to the United States. In the spring of 1907, three police dogs could be seen patrolling the streets of South Orange, New Jersey. In October 1907, dogs and their handlers began patrols in New York City.

The Baltimore Police Department in Maryland

Soon, American cities began to use police dogs. This photo is from 1912 in New York.

organized the first successful K-9 unit. Baltimore's first program failed in 1917 due to lack of training. But that did not stop the city's police from trying again. In 1956, a newspaper article about the use of police dogs in London caught the attention of the department. Soon after, Baltimore police were offered two dogs that already had some training. After several months of further training, the dogs and their handlers were assigned to the streets just two nights a week. They patrolled the areas of the city with the most crime. Just six weeks later, the program was considered a success in improving public safety. By February 1960, Baltimore's outstanding program had grown to forty-five dogs and handlers. Baltimore even built its own training center in 1967.

Other American cities had used working police

K-9 Training Center

The city of Baltimore is well known for its K-9 training center. It is not surprising that police representatives from all over the United States, as well as other countries, have visited the center. Many police departments travel to the center in Maryland to have their K-9 units trained by this outstanding facility.

dogs, but Baltimore was the first to set up an organized program. It is the oldest K-9 program in the country.

The value of police dogs is still very important today. Police dogs can perform duties their human partners cannot. A keen sense of smell helps dogs sniff out smells that a human nose will miss. Supersensitive ears allow dogs to hear sounds that people never would. Terrific vision helps these animals to see at night. They are also skilled at detecting moving objects. Endurance keeps these animals running long distances and for long periods of time. It is no wonder the use of K-9 units continues to grow all around the country.

Chapter 2

Police Dog Breeds

German shepherds are the favorite dog breed for police patrol work. Another popular breed is the Malinois, a type of Belgian shepherd. Both of these breeds are considered working dogs. They have been used by police departments for many years.

A keen sense of smell makes these dogs suitable for police work. This is important for following human scents and sniffing out narcotics or dangerous drugs.

Belgian Malinois is one breed of dog that makes for a great police dog.

Other strong traits include their high energy and drive. When on duty for long hours they will not tire easily. German shepherds and Belgian Malinois are loyal dogs. They will give their lives to protect their handlers. They have the ability to work in both hot and cold weather. These breeds are also very smart and willing to learn. This makes them easy to train. Compared to other breeds, they often have a longer working life.

German shepherds and Belgian Malinois are not the only breeds used in police work. Labrador

Male Dogs vs. Female Dogs

Police departments are more likely to use male dogs than female dogs. Male dogs are more aggressive than female dogs. That means they will not hesitate to attack when given the command. Male dogs also tend to be larger, giving them an advantage against criminals.

retrievers and golden retrievers are also popular choices. But other breeds can be trained as well.

Many wonderful breeds have proven themselves to be useful to police over the years. One expert says that a dog's desire to work is more important than the dog's breed or where the dog comes from.

Some breeds that make good police dogs are the German shepherd, Labrador retriever, and the golden retriever.

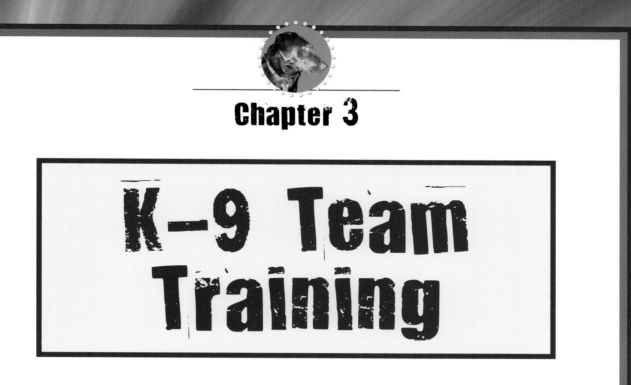

Chapter 3

K-9 Team Training

The Trainer

Dogs and the officers who handle them must go to school to earn K-9 team certification. Training takes place at a training center by a certified trainer. It is the trainer's job to teach both dog and handler how to become successful police partners. Not just anyone can be a police dog trainer. Trainers must have handler experience too.

The dog handler must groom the dog each day. This helps the handler and dog become closer.

The Handlers

Handlers for police K-9 programs are chosen with care. These men and women need to be hardworking and dedicated people.

Most police dogs live with their handlers. This means the officer is also responsible for caring for the dog all the time. When at home, the officer must walk, feed, and care for their K-9 partner just like any other family pet. For this reason, officers and their families should love dogs.

Officers interested in becoming handlers need to be in good physical shape. They must be able to keep up with their high-energy dogs. That is no easy task!

The Dogs

Many successful police dogs have been adopted from animal shelters. In some cases, people give dogs to the police department. Dogs are also purchased from breeders. No matter the source, training starts when the dogs are young. The best age for police dogs to start training is between one and two years old.

Training

Handlers and dogs are matched according to their personalities. The pair must be able to get along if they are going to work well as partners. First-time

handlers and first-time police dogs will learn together. During the learning process, the K-9 team forms a strong bond of trust and friendship.

A reward system is often used to train police dogs. Each time a task is performed well, the dog is rewarded. Rewards can be in the form of praise from the handler or playtime with a favorite toy. A dog may need to repeat a task several times before getting it right. The handler must be patient. In order to learn, it is important that the dog is having fun.

Training begins when the dogs are puppies. This is a German shepherd puppy.

Like people, some dogs may take longer to learn than others. If a dog does not pass the first time, he can always try for certification again. Many police dogs are trained in more than one area. Some examples of other certifications are search and rescue, and narcotics, accelerants, and explosives detection. Training can sometimes take up to eighteen weeks.

While there are many K-9 training schools, most use similar methods. K-9 teams usually are trained and tested in the following areas:

The handler and dog do different training exercises. This dog is practicing jumping out a pretend car window.

Obedience

Obedience is how well the dog obeys the handler. The handler uses verbal and hand signals to give commands to the dog. The dog is tested both on and off a leash. Some examples of commands the handler might use are "sit," "stay," "heel," and "down."

Agility

Agility is how well the dog is able to handle different obstacles. One example of an obstacle is a fence. An obstacle course is used to measure the dog's ability to climb, jump, and crawl. These are all tasks police dogs might have to do in police work.

Scent Work

A police dog must be able to search a certain area and retrieve an article, like a weapon, with a human scent on it. This is called an article search. Police dogs are often called on to search for missing persons.

They are trained to search large areas, like the woods. They should also be able to search within a smaller area, like a yard. These are called area searches. The K-9 team also learns how to search different types of buildings, like warehouses or barns. This is called a building search. During each of these searches, items are hidden for the team to find with the dog using scent as a clue.

Criminal Apprehension

A police dog should show ability to obey the handler's commands when a fleeing suspect is involved. When commanded, the dog should chase and attack a fleeing suspect to aid in apprehension. In some cases, the dog is commanded to stop the chase and return to the handler's side. After a police dog has attacked, he is also trained to release the suspect on command. The dog will then guard the suspect. Criminal

One part of training is scent work. During a training exercise, this dog has just found a container that may contain narcotics.

apprehension is practiced both with and without gunfire. A police dog is also trained to stand guard while the handler searches the suspect. Most important is the dog's willingness to protect the officer from any assault.

These are all tasks police dogs will need to use on the job. To the dogs, these tasks are games. The games continue to be played throughout a police dog's working life.

Handlers and their dogs continue to train even after they are certified. Many attend monthly training sessions. They may even practice during or after work. Officers may take their dogs on trips to the mall or to visit a school. This helps the dogs get used to being around people. It also helps them to be comfortable in different surroundings.

On and off the job, handlers and their dogs work very hard together to stay certified. As a team, most are retested every six months or every year for patrol work and for each certified specialty. Once certified, the crime-fighting K-9 duo is ready to hit the streets!

Chapter 4

Police Dogs on the Job

On the job, a police dog wears a reflective vest. This identifies him as a member of law enforcement. He may also wear a badge. A police dog will always wear some type of collar. A bulletproof vest is also kept handy. The vest will only be used if the handler thinks it may be necessary. The police dog's uniform sends a message to the dog that the team is going to work.

A police dog rides in style in the backseat of a specially designed K-9 vehicle. A special insert serves as a kennel. A soft mat lines the kennel for comfort. The mat also keeps the dog from sliding around. The rear windows are tinted to keep the sun out. Metal guards line these same windows in order to prevent curious people from sticking their fingers in when the windows are rolled down. A special cooling system may also be used so that the car does not become too hot for the dog. A police vehicle may also have another neat feature. The officer can open the rear door of the vehicle by pushing a button on his or her belt. So, in an emergency, the dog can leave the vehicle to assist the officer.

Police dogs wear uniforms, too! Storm, a bomb-sniffing dog with the New York Police Department, is wearing a special badge.

When working, police dogs accompany their handlers on patrol. They may patrol on foot or in

Police dogs get a special spot in the police car. The back seat in some cars is specially designed just for the dog.

their K-9 vehicle. The police dog's main responsibility is to protect. The dog is trained to protect the handler and other officers.

Police dogs aid their handlers in many ways. One

way is their presence. A dog's presence alone can help control a crowd of people. A would-be criminal who sees a dog is less likely to commit a crime.

Police dogs will use their super senses to help search places like streets, yards, and buildings. This is how missing people are often found and lives are saved. And that is not all. Police officers can use some dogs during traffic stops. The dog may sniff a car if narcotics are suspected. This helps police keep dangerous substances off the street. Other times, police dogs are asked to find lost or stolen property. Weapons, like guns or knives, may be used in crimes. Police dogs can find weapons before they fall into the wrong hands. Police dogs often recover evidence that can be used in court to convict people of crimes. If necessary, police dogs can even help in the apprehension of suspects. These are just a few jobs police dogs perform.

Police dogs are also used in airports.

On the scene, police dogs sniff for evidence.

The dog and handler work together to form a crime-fighting team. But when off-duty, police dogs are part of the officer's family. Police dogs and their handlers are often called into action even when they are not on duty. That is why police officers take both the police vehicles and their dogs home with them. The K-9 team's job is to answer calls for help at any time, on or off duty.

Chapter 5

When Police Dogs Retire

t is time for a police dog to retire when the handler sees that the dog is tiring easily or is no longer able to perform the required duties. When a police dog retires, it means the dog no longer works on a K-9 team. This also can be due to an illness or injury. In other cases, retirement could happen when the dog can no longer pass the certification test.

K-9 Dino has just retired! His handler holds retirement papers. Dino was a police dog for eight years and will live with his handler.

The working life of a police dog depends on the dog, but most of these hardworking dogs retire from police work between age eight and ten years old. This is due to the dog's difficult work and the physical effects it has on the dog.

Retired police dogs are offered to their handlers to adopt. In almost all cases, these retired working dogs will live out the rest of their lives at home with their handlers. After all, the handler has been the dog's partner for almost his whole life. In rare cases, the dog may retire to a police department kennel.

Just like people, police dogs may need some time to adapt to retired life. And while "man's best friend" adjusts to restful days at home, the officer is often back at work training a new K-9 partner.

Chapter 6

Police Dogs Are Heroes

Time and again, police dogs have proven themselves to be heroes. A hero is someone who shows great bravery. Many lost children will turn up under the nose of these amazing animals. Criminals will be convicted based on evidence police dogs will find. Assisting in the apprehension of criminals helps make a community a safer place to live. Police dogs demonstrate courage and loyalty.

As members of police departments, these brave dogs may sometimes give their lives in the line of duty.

But what some people might not know is that police dogs have more than one role. While they serve as partners, they also serve as friends.

"I talk to my K-9 Lucky and tell him everything," Officer Shawn Meade says.

"I believe Lucky is truly my best friend and I know that he feels the same toward me."

K-9 police dogs
are truly heroes!

GLOSSARY

accelerant—A material used to start or increase the spread of fire.

apprehension—Arresting a suspect for doing something against the law.

breeders—People who raise certain types of dogs.

convict—To find guilty.

explosive—Something that is likely to explode.

illegal—Against the law.

K-9—Nickname for a police dog, from the word "canine," which means "dog."

narcotics—Dangerous drugs.

obstacle—Something that stands in the way.

vehicle—Transport, such as a car or truck, for people or goods.

LEARN MORE

Books

Knudsen, Shannon. *Police Officers*. Minneapolis, Minn.: Lerner Publications, 2005.

Luke, Melinda. *Helping Paws: Dogs That Serve*. New York: Scholastic, 2001.

Miller, Marie-Therese. *Police Dogs*. New York: Chelsea Clubhouse, 2007.

Presnall, Judith Janda. *Police Dogs*. San Diego, Calif.: Kidhaven Press, 2002.

Internet Addresses

American Humane Association
  <http://www.americanhumane.org>

Natural History Museum
  <http://www.nhm.org/exhibitions/dogs>

Working Dog Foundation K-9 Kids Korner
  <http://www.nhlgc.org/LGCWebsite/WDF/kids_
  korner.htm>

Index